Let's Get Social

by K. Lee

KLEPub.com

Copyright

Published by Krystal Lee Enterprises (KLE Publishing) Copyright ©
2024 by K. Lee All rights reserved.
Please send comments and questions:
Krystal Lee Enterprises
services@KLEPub.com
sales@KLEPub.com

To Reach the Author:
Email: me@authorklee.com or me@drkrystallee.com
Web: AuthorKLee.com
Social Media: @AuthorKLee
770-240-0089 Ext. 1

Printed in the United States of America.
All rights reserved. No part of this book may be reproduced or transmitted in any form or by any means, electronic or mechanical, including photocopying, recording, or any information storage and retrieval system without written permission of the publisher except for brief quotations used in reviews, written specifically for inclusion in a newspaper, blog, magazine, or academic paper.

ISBN: 978-1-945066-57-3

Dedication

We are all people born with a story. Too often, we become politically correct and lose sight of our humanity. I wrote this book to encourage the world to see people as people.

Thank you to my family, children, friends, and the readers of this book. I especially want to thank Yashua for the idea.

Happy reading!

"Hi, students, and welcome to Social Studies! I am your teacher, Mrs. White, and I like to make Social Studies personal and memorable. I think one of the biggest challenges to teaching and learning any subject is seeing how a subject is relevant to both the teacher and the student. Would you agree?

The students were a bit taken aback by the teacher's speech. They were not used to a teacher asking them any questions on the first day of class. They were expecting her to tell them the ground rules. For example, " No talking when I am talking. Follow instructions, be sure to complete assignments, ask for a pass to leave the class, and of course, the all-time favorite, study for every test, or you will fail my class!"

This teacher was different, however. She came off with an inviting tone as if she wanted to have a conversation that lasted the entire semester--or at least for this class. We all know some teachers have a few tricks up their sleeves. So the students played it cool, smiled, and said nothing.

Mrs. White, sensing their hesitation, takes a different approach. She asks the class, "How about we take role? Ok, when I say your name, please raise your hand and let me know you're here."

"Can Caitlin raise your hand for me?"
"Yes, I am here," replies Caitlin.
"Great. Can Liam let me know you are here."
"I'm here, Mrs. White," he replies.
"Francisca?"
"I'm here, Mrs. White," she replies.
"Martin, you are where?"
"That will be me," says Martin.
"Aurora, you are sitting where?"
"Right here, Mrs. White," says Aurora.
"Isabella, are you here?"
"Yup, that's me," she replies.
" Hector, are you with us?"
"Si, that is me," replies Hector.
"So that means you two are Miriam and Walter." The two nod in unison.

7

"Great, I am glad to see we are all here. So now, getting back to the conversation. I want to let you know I have a conversational approach to teaching. I think a lot can be retained when you have a conversation with someone, and they are interested in the subject matter. But for us to gauge one another, I think the first ground rule I want to share is for us to be honest."

"When I ask you a question, I would like an honest answer. Yes, I do want you to be mindful of your language as well as be respectful when you share, but honesty is the best policy. I know asking hand-raising questions might be the best for starting this class, but as we progress, more questions, I am sure, will surface, and I welcome those conversations when they arise."

"The first question is an easy one. Raise your hand if you see a white person in this room." The students burst out laughing and started looking at each other with astonishment.

"I meant it. Be honest. Do you see white people in this room?" The students whisper among themselves for a little bit longer, and then Liam speaks.

"Mrs. White, of course, there are white people in this room. No one really asks that question out loud. I mean, we mark it on forms, of course, but it just sounds strange to say it out loud."

"I can agree with that. It sounds strange to say it out loud." Mrs. White replies. "However, I disagree with you that there are white people in this room." The entire class has eyes the size of pool balls as they glare at Mrs. White, puzzled.

"Is anyone going to ask me the obvious question?" Mrs. White inquires. Without further hesitation, Miriam says, "How is it that you are an adult and don't know there are white people in this room? I mean, I don't mean to be disrespectful, but even you have white skin."

"Really, you think I have white skin? Second question: do you think people are to be defined by the hue of their skin?"

Walter replies, "Why do you sound like Martin Luther King? I mean, who in this 21st Century doesn't understand race? I mean, I would never say a whole lot of stuff because it just isn't appropriate, but you seem totally okay asking if white people are in this room. Aren't you white?"

"That is the question. This is our first lesson. Welcome to this series, "Let's Get Social," Mrs. White writes the title on the board, and she turns to face the students. Her face makes an inquisitive smile, and she says, "Can we know a person by the color of their skin? Walter brought up Martin Luther King Jr., a great man and contributor to society. Raise your hand if you agree for me, please."

Every student raises their hand without hesitation. "Good, so we all have working hands, and we appear to agree on this matter. Now, I want everyone to raise their hands if you see a white person in this room." Again, without hesitation, the entire class raises their hands.

"The class agrees again. Wonderful. This uniformity and understood agreement is what we call social norms."

"Raise your hand if you believe black people are in this room?" The students no longer laugh at her questions; they are curious about what she is leading. As expected, however, the entire class raises their hands, identifying black people in the room.

Her third question is similar, "Okay, how many people in this room would say Spanish people are in this room?" Without hesitation, the entire class raises their hands, and Mrs. White smiles.

"Okay, I think we are all going to enjoy our series and learn something great about each other. Aren't you all curious why I asked you these three questions?"

The students all speak and say "yes." Mrs. White responds, "Great! Then you will look forward to my next class. Please read your assigned reading for tonight, and we will continue our conversation on tomorrow."

"Really, you are going to leave us hanging like this," says Aurora. "Hey, come on, you know this is messed up. You have to give us something!" says Miriam in a joking manner.

"Okay, I will tell you this. After this series, 'Let's Get Social,' I want to ask each of you if you see White, Black, Spanish, or even Asian people in this room. I think the responses are going to be a conversation you will have for the rest of your lives."

Let's Get Social

Leaving the classroom, the students truly looked forward to that night's homework. They weren't sure what they would be learning in class the next day, and the book didn't seem to give much of a hint. What they read was what they expected: a dry book that attempts to make learning history fun.

The biggest problem was that the student simply wasn't that interested in the content. Making history relationally and personable, the children agreed, could make learning more bearable, but they all doubted it could be made fun.

They all also questioned whether they would talk about a topic most people ignore all of their lives. Certainly, filling out forms has never been a social topic in any of their lives up to this point. Most conversations the students found interesting were about life matters, trends, and even fads that would be outdated tomorrow. But at least they captured their attention for today.

Mrs. White dared to offer an alternative to the status quo.

In with the new and out with the old is just the way life goes. The teacher, I am sure, thought, how can you make the old hold just as much value as the new if those hearing the information were not interested?

Funny thing, they were interested. They couldn't stop thinking and talking about the class. What will she show them that they didn't know? They pondered.

"Isn't white and black people super basic social constructs since the beginning of time? Every social studies class thus far, including the Civil War, can be understood to include black and white people.

Was life really ever intended to be understood in shades of color? Were we meant to erase and subtract a person's culture, history, language, and beliefs, then bottle those differences in a jar, and afterward proceed with shaping their existence by a simple color?

Is it fair to the world that it would appear that nations and peoples have done just that? We have many stereotypes for people and nations, with very few facts about what we know today as facts have come about.

I encourage you to explore these concepts and consider how you also see people, languages, and the world around you. You just may be shocked at how these ideas have shaped your world, like the people in this book. Let's read on, shall we?

The noise buzzed around the room as Mrs. White entered the classroom, excited about today's lesson. She asks the first question they all want to know, "What is the first thing we need to get down to some truths?"

Puzzled, they look at each other. Then Liam says, "The Internet?"

Mrs. White replies I can see how you would think that. During your young years, the idea of going to a library is probably not as important to you as it was for me growing up. We didn't have everything a fingertip away."

"During my youth, we didn't have the internet, and no, before you ask, I am not likely as old as your grandmother. Not too many years ago, books were a thing. I mean, it's a real big thing! If you wanted to learn anything, you had to be willing to pick up a book. I want to share some books with you today. Before you groan, it will be tons of fun!"

The students are reluctant, and they put away their things and place their backpacks either underneath their desks or dangle behind their chairs. They turn forward as Mrs. White plops the many books in her hand on the desk.

Have you ever heard the saying that history is his story? I want you to consider a trend I noticed in history. There is nothing new under the sun. In government, during times of war, and even in social constructs, people have similarities in every nation.

I want us to explore these similarities and then see how the commonalities we share can help us better understand one another. Are we all familiar with the Greeks and the Romans? Did you know that when the Greeks lost to the Romans, their culture was wrapped in or absorbed by the Romans?

Consider this: because the Greeks had a culture and social norm that the Romans wanted to use, they only made adjustments to their culture.

Or if you have ever played the game telephone, I might show you my age on that one. You will find a similar truth. History is told from the perspective of those who have the last say. Those with the last word tend to teach your children and the coming generations.

Something I want to show you is that, in light of us all getting to know each other, I thought I would take a personal approach to presenting the information you all have to learn. Would you agree if we can make social studies relatable, we can better remember history? Furthermore, it is my prayer that we don't duplicate our history.

Raising your hands, is there a moment in history you would say was terrible? All the children raised their hands. Mrs. White looked over the class for several seconds and said, "I am glad you are all aware that we have been through some terrible times as people. Now tell me, who here thinks life moving forward could improve?

"I want you all to take a moment to see life from my perspective, and I will also see life from yours. I want us to discuss what we believe and how we feel about the evidence. We won't agree on everything, but that is okay."

"However, please keep in mind that in this classroom, we are to respect each other. Some topics are just hard, but they are history. We can not learn how to move forward if we are too afraid to look backward. Everybody agrees?"

The class nods yet again, and Mrs. White takes her seat. She asks the class what they would like to learn first. The room is quiet, and no one says a thing. Mrs. White allows the silence to linger in the room. She loves the anticipation.

She then says, "Okay, no one has ideas of what they would like to learn as it pertains to history. How about your family? I know your names, and that's about it. Tell me where you were born, which country your family originated in, and if there is anything unique you would like to share."

The class is still silent, although the student's eyes are circling the room. It is as if there is a social code not to speak first, so they await their names being called. Mrs. White, knowing the class needs to press on, calls out, "Isabella, please tell me a little about yourself."

Isabella shifts her body to the right as she sits in her chair. She takes a deep breath and swings her feet back under her chair with her toes pointed to the floor. If the students could see her hands, they would know she was pinching her left index finger.

"I want to ask since we do live in America, and learning American history is important to people who live here or desire to immigrate. What all do you know about American History?"

Isabella answered, "This country was founded by people who came here from Great Britain. They colonized here and worked with the Native Americans when they arrived."

She continued to say, "Then, ultimately, they expanded, creating the fifty original states over time and taking on more territories. Today, the United States of America connects many states and territories, even in other countries, to form the country and the people. We are a melting pot for all cultures."

"Very good, you nailed a good version of the American story. Who else can help us understand American history?"

Miriam raises her hand, and she is called on, "I heard the Americans killed the Indians and took their land." Walter raises his hand, "I think there were slaves here."

Hector says, "Some of the United States was taken from Mexico and Spain."

Martin says, "Black people came here on ships. But we weren't always slaves. We were kings before here."

"No, we sent missionaries to help in other countries with food, making shelter, and improving life," replies Caitlin.

"I am not sure what history you have read or if you also think Christopher Columbus was great, look at history again," replied Francisca.

"Yes, I can see the passion you all have about what you know about history."

"I pray we are not going to learn the same thing over and over again. It's boring learning about the same people every year." Said Liam.

"I couldn't agree with you more. So what would you like to learn more about?"

"Slavery," says Miriam.

"Okay," replies Mrs. White. "And why do you want to learn more about slavery?"

"Well, I don't know much about it. I only know what I have been told, and that is all black people were slaves working to pick cotton in the South."

"Interesting."

"No, black people came here on slave ships because they were captured by white people and stolen," replied Martin.

"What else do we know about slavery?" Mrs. White looks around the room, and Walter says, "Y'all are saying white people stole black people? I heard black people sold black people to white people."

"I heard white people brought bibles and stole land," says Miriam.

"Wow, okay," replied Mrs. White. "Seems like we have a lot to say about this topic."

"Honestly, I don't know what you all are talking about. Nobody was stolen, but they immigrated here like everyone else. Yes, they didn't get the same jobs and had to work hard because they didn't know how to do other stuff," replied Caitlin.

"Please tell me she is joking," replied Miriam.

"Okay, we are going to respect each other, and I think we need to unpack this subject a lot more. So this will be your first assignment."

"I want you all to select three sources to read from my list and tell me what you learned about slavery and the people. I want to be clear: slavery didn't happen out of thin air, so we will explore the origins of slavery and any routes of passage that permitted the transport of black people.

I think you will find something very interesting about people."

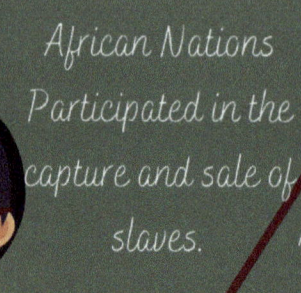

African Nations Participated in the capture and sale of slaves.

Did you know?

Most of the slaves didn't end up in the US or Britain but in Brazil.

Over 4 million slaves were brought to the Caribbean and this location was a main hub that surpassed Brazil with selling the most slave laborers.

"Portugal, Britain, Spain, France, the Netherlands, the United States, and Denmark were the seven most active countries in the slave trade. Smaller countries like Sweden and other European nations also played a part."

The Middle East participated in the slave trade for centuries, with sultanates driving the trade in East Africa, buying and selling slaves from Russia to Africa. Merchants from the Arabian peninsula and Persia bought slaves from the Horn of Africa and the Swahili coast, then traded them to the Indian subcontinent.

Other helpful facts about the Trans-Atlantic Slave Trade.

- During the Transatlantic slave trade, which lasted over 300 years, enslaved Africans were taken to many countries, including Brazil, Britain, The United States, the Caribbean, Guyanas, Cuba, and North America!
- Brazil - 41% of Africans disembarked in Brazil, which is home to the largest population of African descendants outside of Africa today.
- British American ports - 29% of Africans disembarked in British American ports, including the Caribbean, the United States, and the Guyanas.
- Spanish America - 11% of Africans disembarked in Spanish America, including the Spanish island of Cuba, where the last slave ship arrived in the late 1860s.
- North America - 4% of Africans disembarked in North America, where a rigid color line separated Black and white people.
- Angola was a major source of slaves, with European traders loading African captives at many points along the African coast, including Angola, and transporting them to the Americas. Luanda, Angola's largest slave port, supplied at least 1.6 million people to the Americas, with most ending up in Brazil.

Reading List To Explore!

Here are some people, titles, subjects, and books to research that can help you take the journey with my students to discover what became of the many millions of slaves that were sold over a 300-year span throughout the world. Our world today was heavily influenced by the Trans-Atlantic Slave Trade. Let's explore how.

- True-Born Maroons - Kenneth Bilby
- Black Spartacus: The Epic Life of Toussaint Louverture - Sudhir Hazareesingh
- Njinga Mbande - Queen of Angola
- The Atlantic Slave Trade
- Hidden Colors
- Harriet Tubman
- The Interesting Narrative of the Life of Olaudah Equiano
- Mahommah Gardo Baquaqua
- Hebrews to Negros

The students started their reading, and Mrs. White thought it was a good idea to allow the class to form their own groups of three to discuss the material. During the group conversations, the students found the subject to be more relatable, and they asked to present in groups.

Mrs. White thought it was a great idea!

Group one is ready to present! Miriam, Hector, and Aurora come up before the class, bubbling with excitement. They line up and whip out their poster board to present!

Miriam clears her throat to ensure she has the attention of the room before she begins. "Friends, my group: Aurora, Hector, and I are excited to be here and present to you the life of Toussaint Louverture! His last name, Louverture, means "opening," and he selected it himself. The true reason was not known, but I think it was because he opened the door wide open for the people of Haiti to be set free. He was essentially a Moses of his country who helped to set many slaves free!--and he scared the French and the British because of his ability to lead a war and win again and again. There is no doubt he had something. I think God was blessing him."

Aurora says, "Toussaint Louverture was born in 1743 in modern-day Haiti. He was taught French and Creole by his father, a slave. He had many titles working on the plantation, and these jobs helped to set his heart on freedom! He developed a military mindset, was a Catholic in practice, and did not practice voodoo, nor did he encourage it.

It is believed he was a disciplined man who was a strict vegetarian. He was not perfect, and his actions can easily be misunderstood. He was brilliant in battle, so much so that the French used him to help them fight the British on French soil. He was also helpful in fighting to liberate many parts of Haiti and training warriors to defend it using gorilla warfare.

He was a dangerous man because he could lead people in battle and restore people's dignity."

33

The final speaker, Hector, closes the presentation by saying, "He was legally freed in 1776, secured his name, got married, and had two sons. As a military commander, he fought and conquered the land of Hispaniola, and he appointed himself as the general for life with near absolute power.

It is not clear if he made this rule to protect the people or his self-interest, some would argue; however, during the war, it is easy to understand that accidents, deaths, and many lives are lost too often before resolution is reached. He was blamed for many deaths but also accounted for saving many slaves. He helped negotiate a peace treaty so that he would not invade Jamaica and (currently) the Dominican Republic.

He helped to organize peace in the land--not perfectly, but his plans and guidance made many slaves free and kept them free since the Haitian Revolution. He returned to France by request and was arrested and interrogated--likely tortured until he died in 1803. Toussaint is still regarded as a hero of Haiti and a champion for God."

"Wow, thank you three so much. I believe we all enjoyed learning about Toussaint Louverture! I want you all to take a moment and write down any questions you have. We will discuss them at the end of all presentations for the sake of time."

She looks toward the remaining two groups and says, "Can I have the next group stand up, please, and walk to the front of the class? You can decide, and if you can't, I will select."

The two groups hesitated for a moment but then settled on Liam, Caitlin, and Francisca as the group that went next. They shuffled to the front of the class to present their board.

"Hi everyone. I am Caitlin, and I am excited to introduce my amazing group, Liam and Francisca. We picked to talk about Harriet Tubman, an influential African American woman. Harriet was affectionally known as 'Black Moses' and helped to free many slaves. She ran away, securing her own freedom in 1849, but suffered greatly before doing so. Her only regret was not to save more. She retired in a home for elderly African Americans that she built years prior. She had a servant's heart all her life."

Francisca chimes in, "Harriet Tubman, born as Minty, was believed to be born in 1822. She died in 1913, just a few short years after the Roaring 20s.

Harriet didn't have an easy life as a slave. Her mother and father were wed, and she had nine brothers and sisters. Three of her sisters were sold early on, and her brother Moses was to be sold also, but her mother hid him and threatened to bash anybody's head that came into her house to get him! Needless to say, that sale was canceled, and that event sparked a flame within the young Harriet.

Harriet was hired for several jobs starting at the age of 6. Being a child, she made mistakes and was beaten for failing; she carried the markings on her body. She was once accidentally hit in the head by a heavy metal object that busted her skull open. She laid in pain for two days without medical attention, and this injury-plagued her the rest of her life."

Liam looks up from his paper and says, "She was often sick, and because she proved to be of less use after she was married and growing older, her owner thought to sell her. She didn't desire to be sold, so she prayed that God would change his heart. When that didn't happen, she prayed he would die instead. Shortly after, he died, and she faced her fear yet again, being sold. It was then that she decided to run.

After she completed her mission of freedom, she wanted to save her family-- and she did! She went on at least 13 missions to Maryland to help her siblings, parents, and other slaves who heard her beloved song. She was believed to either know God or speak to a mysterious being that led her on her expeditions. She did carry a gun and was not afraid to use it on anyone.

She used the Underground Railroad, a network of free blacks and white abolitionists, to travel to Philadelphia and, in later years, Canada. She supported the Union and became a spy. It was a well-suited job because she was easy to overlook. No one would have thought an ill woman would be capable of all that she accomplished. Harriet is an American hero and saint if a title could ever be fit to me."

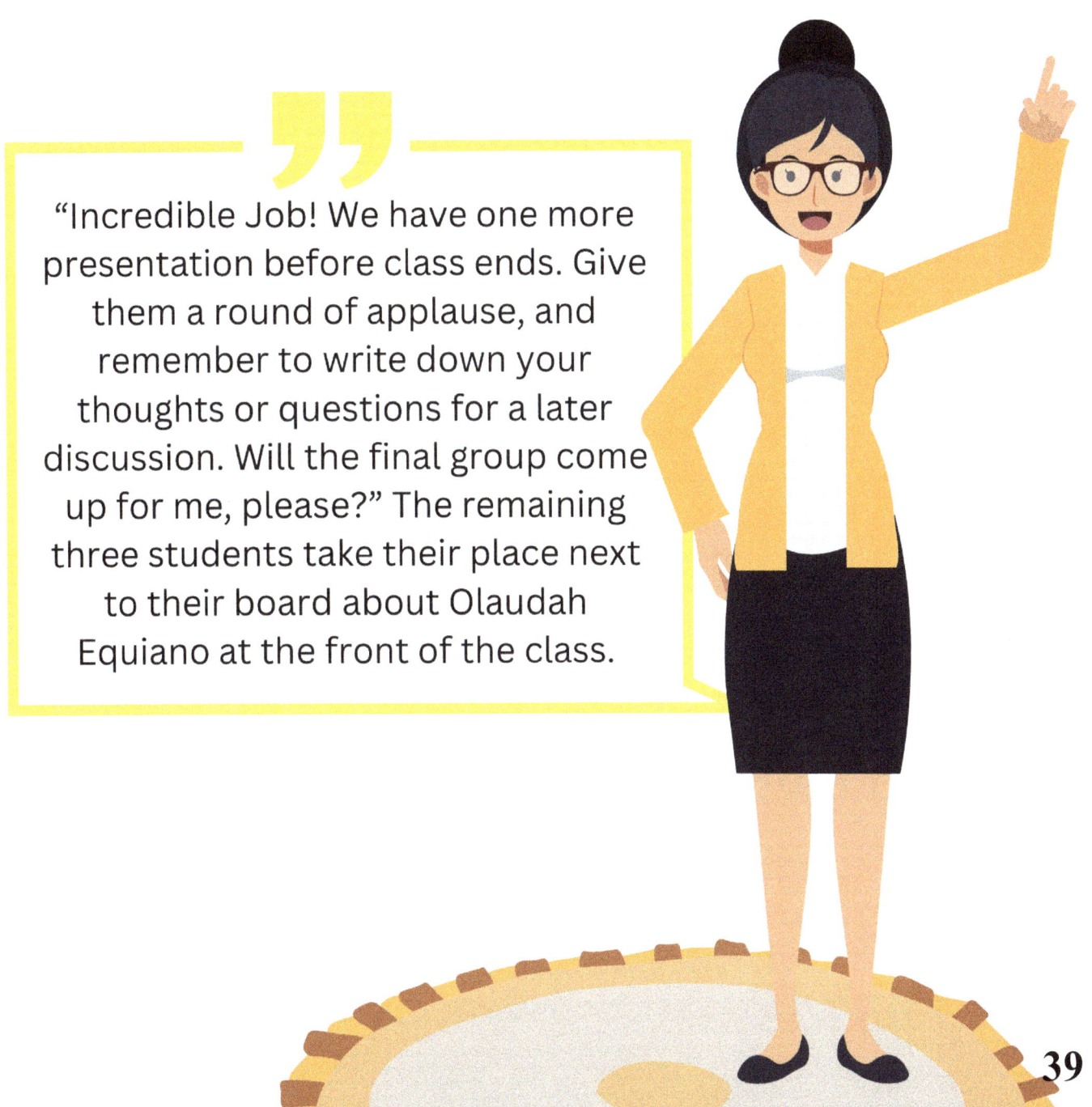

"Incredible Job! We have one more presentation before class ends. Give them a round of applause, and remember to write down your thoughts or questions for a later discussion. Will the final group come up for me, please?" The remaining three students take their place next to their board about Olaudah Equiano at the front of the class.

Walter speaks first, "Olaudah Equiano was a man born in what would be today Nigeria. He was captured with his sister and sold to a Navy Officer in the Caribbean. He was bought and sold two more times before purchasing his own freedom in 1766. As a free man in the 1780s, he began to get involved with the British Abolitionist movement.

Olaudah's contribution to the literary world helped to shine a much-needed light on slavery. His biography sold so well and gained so much attention that he had nine installments. His work helped to pave the way for the British Slave Act of 1807, which abolished slavery.

His name changed every time he was bought and sold. He could only use his birth name in his writings. His fourth owner saw that he was smart, and using him to carry gunpowder seemed too simple of a task. So, he sent him to school in London to learn to read and write.

Isabella picks up the baton and says, "While in London, he was baptized, although he was a Christian since he was 14 years old. Although he could read and write, this was for the benefit of his owner and not self-preservation. He was working on a ship for him and was taught how to trade for his own account by his owner. This owner allowed him to buy his freedom for 40 pounds. When he purchased his freedom, he desired for him to be his business partner, but he refused when he was almost kidnapped and taken again."

Martin jumps in and says, "He knew his purpose was bigger than slavery, but it did include slavery. He got involved with the abolitionist movement and wrote several writings. Quakers and other people supported him as part of the movement. He was heavily encouraged to write his story, and with financial support, publication, and promotion provided he could. Equiano did get married and had two daughters. He died a year after his wife died (1796) in 1797. There might be controversy over his writings, but one thing that is not arguable is his impact on the lives of many people living in Britain. He was an advocate for the Black Community and a voice they trusted. Some would call him a hero."

"Class, I have to tell you I am impressed with your reports and how well you responded to this assignment. I want to ask if anyone has something to share about a presentation you heard today?" It was a joy to see the children raise their hands to ask questions.

Questions

- Was slavery only happening in America?
- Who did you find to have the most impactful story?
- Do you feel like using words like "Black" is a good idea?
- What did you learn from this book?
- What will you remember most about one of the three presentations?
- Who had your favorite presentation?
- How do you feel you can impact the world?
- Do you feel that after hearing the stories in this book, you are encouraged to do something big with your life also?
- What career path are you excited to learn more about?
- Which book will you read from the list, or what other people do you want to look up?
- Which country had the most enslaved people?
- Do you think that slavery lasted too long?
- What grade would you give each group for their presentation?

"This is what I wanted you all to see. Yes, there might be traumatic experiences that have happened in people's lives that you have heard today. But all of them demonstrated their power, self-worth, and influence in their own special way. We didn't learn about slaves. We learned about heroes, veterans, missionaries, and people who made their dreams come true! I want you to think about something you want to impact in the world--no matter what it is, and write it down."

"We have heard about situations that seem hopeless for change, but the impossible happened for each of them. I want you all to tell me when you hear these stories, do you honestly see these people as black? Or can you see them as Haitian, Nigerian, and African American? It is when we can see people for who they are that we can pave a better future forward for us all. How we see each other confirms or changes our future."

The bell rang at that moment, politely given enough time for Mrs. White to complete her thought. The students don't move. They are still glued to their seats.

Mrs. White continues, "I know we all have to leave, but this is my expectation for this class. I would like for you all to commit to seeing the people we study as who they are and not what they are first.

I look forward to us journeying through the upcoming months, and I haven't forgotten. I will tell you more about my history and ancestry as well. Up next is Hispanic heritage, and I trust you will join me in that lesson prepared to learn and have fun!

See you on Monday for class. Have a wonderful weekend!"

Dr. Lee has authored over thirty books across more than seven genres: adult, children, youth fiction, self-help, spiritual growth, novels, business, and empowerment to help people in their most profound times of need.

She is also passionate about coaching programs WAE Process (Write Anything Easily), Embrace Your Crown, Turn Key Solution for Small and New Businesses, Transfrom Go Beyond Change Personal Development, and The Lesson for Youth and Teenagers.

- Connect with me using the QR or visit
- AuthorKLee.com
- Social sites with the handle: AuthorKLee

Resources

Bilby, Kenneth. "True-Born Maroons" *University Press of Florida*. March 2008.

Hazareesingh, Sudhir. "Black Spartacus: The Epic Life of Toussaint Louverture" *MacMillion* September 2021.

Heywood, Linda. "Njinga of Angola: Africa's Warrior Queen" *Harvard University Press* February 2019

Wellman, Billy. "The Atlantic Slave Trade: An Enthralling Overview of European Colonization and Slavery in the New World (Forced Labor in History)" Forced Labor in History Series May 2024

Hidden Colors 1 & 2 Video Series The Untold History of Aboriginal, Moor, and African Decent. DVD or Youtube: Accessed 9/30/2024

Bradford, Sarah "Harriet The Moses of Her People" *Bradford's Classic* October 2020

Olaudah, Equiano "The Interesting Narrative of the Life of Olaudah Equiano: Or Gustavus Vassa, The African, Written By Himself" CreateSpace Independent Publishing Platform September 2015

Law, Robin and Lovejoy, Paul. "The Biography of Mahommah Gardo Baquaqua: His Passage from Slavery to Freedom in Africa and America" *Markus Wiener Publishing* December 2006

Dalton, Ronald. Hebrews to Negros: Wake Up Black America! *G Publishing* May 2015

Shop books by Author K. Lee
If you need a ghostwriter, editor, or want to publish a book visit KLEPub.com or call 770-240-0089 Ext. 1

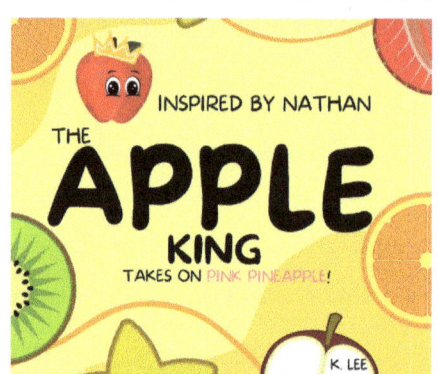

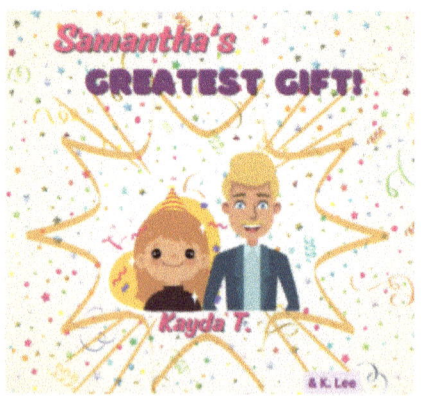

Get Published with KLE Publishing!

If you need a ghostwriter, editor, or want to publish a book visit KLEPub.com or call 770-240-0089 Ext. 1

Order More Books Today!

If you need a ghostwriter, editor, or want to publish a book visit KLEPub.com or call 770-240-0089 Ext. 1

www.ingramcontent.com/pod-product-compliance
Lightning Source LLC
Chambersburg PA
CBHW040003080526
44586CB00027B/2872